CHAMBER MUSIC OF
ROBERT SCHUMANN

Edited by
CLARA SCHUMANN

DOVER PUBLICATIONS, INC.
NEW YORK

Published in Canada by General Publishing Company, Ltd., 30 Lesmill Road, Don Mills, Toronto, Ontario.

Published in the United Kingdom by Constable and Company, Ltd., 10 Orange Street, London WC2H 7EG.

Chamber Music of Robert Schumann, first published in 1981, is a selection of unabridged works from *Serie IV. Für Streichinstrumente* and *Serie V. Für Pianoforte und andere Instrumente* of the Collected Works Edition (*Robert Schumann's Werke. Herausgegeben von Clara Schumann*), originally published by Breitkopf & Härtel, Leipzig, in the following years: 1880 (Trios 1 and 3), 1881 (Quintet, String Quartets), 1885 (Piano Quartet) and 1887 (Trio 2).

The publisher is grateful to the Sibley Music Library of the Eastman School of Music, Rochester, N.Y., for making its material available for reproduction.

International Standard Book Number: 0-486-24101-7
Library of Congress Catalog Card Number: 80-69744

Manufactured in the United States of America
Dover Publications, Inc.
180 Varick Street
New York, N.Y. 10014

CONTENTS

GLOSSARY OF GERMAN TERMS IN TRIOS NOS. 1–3

Am Steg bis zum . . .: close to the bridge (sul ponticello) up to the . . .

ausdrucksvoll: with expression

Bewegt, doch nicht zu rasch: agitatedly, but not too fast

Bewegter: with greater agitation

Erstes Tempo: original tempo

Etwas bewegter: somewhat more agitatedly

Etwas langsamer: somewhat more slowly

etwas zurückhaltend: holding back somewhat

Etwas zurückhaltend bis zum langsameren Tempo: holding back somewhat up to the slower tempo

Im Tempo: in tempo

In mässiger Bewegung: with moderate movement

Kräftig, mit Humor: powerfully and humorously

Langsam, mit inniger Empfindung: slowly, with deep feeling

Lebhaft: vivaciously

Lebhaft, doch nicht zu rasch: vivaciously, but not too fast

markirt: marcato

Mit Energie und Leidenschaft: with energy and passion

Mit Feuer: fierily

Mit innigem Ausdruck: with heartfelt expression

mit Pedal: with pedal

Nach und nach schneller: gradually faster

Nicht zu rasch: not too fast

Rasch: quickly

Rascher: more quickly

Schneller: faster

Sehr lebhaft: very vivaciously

Sehr rasch: very quickly

Tempo I. nur ruhiger: original tempo, but more calmly

Verschiebung bis zum . . .: soft pedal up to the . . .

Ziemlich langsam: rather slowly

QUINTET IN E-FLAT MAJOR, OP. 44
For Two Violins, Viola, Cello and Pianoforte

Trio I.

Trio II.
L'istesso tempo.

QUARTET IN E-FLAT MAJOR, OP. 47
For Violin, Viola, Cello and Pianoforte

SCHERZO.

Tempo I.

Tempo I.

Here the cello tunes the C string a whole tone lower, to B-flat.

cantabile

mf

pizz.

mf

dolce

Ped. ✱ ℞ℰ𝒹.

FINALE.

Vivace. ♩ = 152.

TRIO NO. 1 IN D MINOR, OP. 63

For Violin, Cello and Pianoforte

I.

II.

122   *Piano Trio No. 1 in D Minor*

III.

IV.

142   *Piano Trio No. 1 in D Minor*

144 *Piano Trio No. 1 in D Minor*

Nach und nach schneller.

Nach und nach schneller.

148   *Piano Trio No. 1 in D Minor*

TRIO NO. 2 IN F MAJOR, OP. 80
For Violin, Cello and Pianoforte

I.

162   *Piano Trio No. 2 in F Major*

II.

Mit innigem Ausdruck. M.M. ♩=58.

172   *Piano Trio No. 2 in F Major*

III.

In mässiger Bewegung. M.M. ♩=50.

IV.

188 *Piano Trio No. 2 in F Major*

TRIO NO. 3 IN G MINOR, OP. 110
For Violin, Cello and Pianoforte

I.

194   *Piano Trio No. 3 in G Minor*

II.

Ziemlich langsam. ($\flat$ = 116.)

III.

Sehr rasch.

Sehr rasch.

IV.

Kräftig, mit Humor. ($\quad$ = 104.)

Kräftig, mit Humor. ($\quad$ = 104.)

Mit Pedal.

214   *Piano Trio No. 3 in G Minor*

220 *Piano Trio No. 3 in G Minor*

STRING QUARTET NO. 1 IN A MINOR, OP. 41, NO. 1

226   *String Quartet No. 1 in A Minor*

Scherzo.
Presto. ♩. = 138.

238   *String Quartet No. 1 in A Minor*

242   *String Quartet No. 1 in A Minor*

Tempo I.

STRING QUARTET NO. 2 IN F MAJOR, OP. 41, NO. 2

Andante, quasi Variazioni. ♩. = 69.

250   *String Quartet No. 2 in F Major*

TRIO.
L'istesso tempo.

STRING QUARTET NO. 3 IN A MAJOR, OP. 41, NO. 3

274   *String Quartet No. 3 in A Major*

Quasi Trio.

282   *String Quartet No. 3 in A Major*